Acclaim for C H I N U A   A C H E B E *'s*

Home and Exile

"A moving account of an exceptional life. . . . Achebe reveals the inner workings of the human conscience through the predicaments of Africa and his own intellectual life. . . . A story of the triumph of the mind, told in the words of one of this century's most gifted writers. The book is bound to be a classic of its kind."

—Henry Louis Gates, Jr.

"The book is both a kind of autobiography and a rumination on the power stories have to create a sense of dispossession or to confer strength, depending on who is wielding the pen."   —*The Atlantic Monthly*

"Subtle, witty and gracious . . . one of those small gems of literary and historical analysis that readers will treasure and reread over the years."   —*Publishers Weekly*

"In defining the dignity and vibrancy of African literature, Chinua Achebe defies the stranglehold of colonial, imperialist and cultural dispossession. He brings us into balance with a world of literature and hope that the West with its myth of primacy denies."   —Walter Mosley

"[Achebe's] 1959 debut, *Things Fall Apart*, remains one of the most widely read books in African literature. *Home and Exile*—the author's first book in more than a decade—comes full circle with its look at colonialism's long reach."   —*Emerge*

CHINUA ACHEBE

Home and Exile

Chinua Achebe was born in Nigeria in 1930. He was raised in the large village of Ogidi, one of the first centers of Anglican missionary work in Eastern Nigeria, and is a graduate of University College, Ibadan.

His early career in radio ended abruptly in 1966, when he left his post as Director of External Broadcasting in Nigeria during the national upheaval that led to the Biafran War. He was appointed Senior Research Fellow at the University of Nigeria, Nsukka, and began lecturing widely abroad.

From 1972 to 1976, and again from 1987 to 1988, Mr. Achebe was Professor of English at the University of Massachusetts, Amherst, and also for one year at the University of Connecticut, Storrs.

Cited in the London *Sunday Times* as one of the "1,000 Makers of the Twentieth Century" for defining "a modern African literature that was truly African" and thereby making "a major contribution to world literature," Chinua Achebe has published novels, short stories, essays, and children's books. His volume of poetry, *Christmas in Biafra*, written during the Biafran War, was the joint winner of the first Commonwealth Poetry Prize. Of his novels, *Arrow of God* won the New Statesman–Jock Campbell Award, and *Anthills of the Savannah* was a finalist for the 1987 Booker Prize.

Mr. Achebe has received numerous honors from around the world, including the Honorary Fellowship of the American Academy of Arts and Letters, as well as more than thirty honorary doctorates from universities in England, Scotland, the United States, Canada, Nigeria, and South Africa. He is also the recipient of Nigeria's highest honor for intellectual achievement, the Nigerian National Order of Merit.

Mr. Achebe lives with his wife in Annandale-on-Hudson, New York, where they teach at Bard College. They have four children.

Also by Chinua Achebe

Home and Exile

Chinua Achebe

Anchor Books

A Division of Random House, Inc.

New York

For Anna

FIRST ANCHOR BOOKS EDITION, SEPTEMBER 2001

Copyright © 2000 by Chinua Achebe

All rights reserved under International and Pan-American Copyright
Conventions. Published in the United States by Anchor Books, a division of
Random House, Inc., New York, and simultaneously in Canada by Random
House of Canada Limited, Toronto. Originally published in hardcover in the
United States by Oxford University Press, Inc., New York, in 2000.

Anchor Books and colophon are registered trademarks of
Random House, Inc.

Library of Congress Cataloging-in-Publication Data
Achebe, Chinua.
Home and exile / Chinua Achebe.
p. cm.
Includes bibliographic references and index.
ISBN 0-385-72133-1
1. Achebe, Chinua. 2. Authors, Nigerian—20th century—Biography.
3. Africa—Civilization—Western influences. 4. Nigerians—United
States—Biography. 5. Exiles—Nigeria—Biography.
6. Nigeria—Intellectual life.
I. Title.
PR9387.9.A3 Z467 2001
823'.914—dc21 2001022599
CIP

www.anchorbooks.com

Printed in the United States of America
10 9 8 7 6 5 4 3 2 1

Contents

Preface

This book came out of three lectures that I delivered as the 1998 McMillan-Stewart Lectures at Harvard University on December 9, 10, and 11, 1998. I am grateful to Henry Louis Gates Jr. and his colleagues at the W.E.B. Du Bois Institute for Afro-American Research at Harvard for asking me to give the lectures and for being such attentive hosts to my wife, our son and me on that occasion.

I must thank also my old friends A.K. Appiah of Ghana and Biodun Jeyifo of Nigeria and the young and brilliant Caribbean writer

Patricia Powell for their generous words that primed my presentations. Good introductions always work well for me!

For converting my scribbles into a publisher-ready manuscript I am indebted to Karen Becker, my colleague at Bard College.

Chinua Achebe

Home and Exile

My Home
Under Imperial Fire

One of the earliest memories I can summon from the realm of childhood was a homecoming that was extraordinary even for such recollections. I was returning to my ancestral home for the first time. The paradox of returning for the first time need not detain us now because there are more engaging things at hand. I was five years old and riding in a motor vehicle also for the first time. I had looked forward very much to this experience, but it was not working out right. Sitting in the back of the truck and facing what seemed the wrong way, I could not see where we were going, only where we were coming from. The dust and the smell and the speed and the roadside trees rushing forward as we rushed back finally overcame me with fear and dizziness. I was glad when it all finally came to a halt at my home and my town.

The reason for my frightening journey was that my father, after thirty years in missionary work, founding a new church here and tending a fledgling one there, had earned his rest and a pension of thirty shillings a month and was taking his family to his ancestral home, to a house he had scraped to build in the final years of his evangelism. It was a grand house with an iron roof and whitewashed earth walls, a far cry from the thatch-roofed mission house we had just left.

Of all our family, only my father had ever lived in Ogidi, to which he now brought us, and he had not lived there since he first began teaching for the Anglican Mission in 1904; it was now 1935. My mother, who had served beside him since their marriage five years into his career, had grown up in her own town, twenty-odd miles away.

Soon after our return to Ogidi my father preached a homecoming sermon at St. Philip's Anglican Church, which he had helped to found at the turn of the century. I don't remember the sermon but I do remember one of its consequences. My father had presumably told the congregation something about his missionary journeys that had begun in 1904, and they were so taken with the antiquity of it all that they nicknamed him, there and then, Mister Nineteen-Four, which did not sound to me like an unambiguous encomium. But worse was to come to my siblings and me at school as Nineteen-Four's children. I am not sure why I found the sobriquet as disagreeable as I did. In any event, it helped to fix in my mind the idea that Ogidi people were not very nice and that school was an unfriendly place. My homecoming did not begin too well.

The Igbo people of southeastern Nigeria are more than ten million strong and must be accounted one of the major peoples of Africa. Conventional practice would call them a tribe, but I no longer follow that convention. I call them a nation. "Here we go again!," you might be thinking. Well, let me explain. My Pocket Oxford Dictionary defines tribe as follows: "group of (esp. primitive) families or communities linked by social, religious or blood ties and usually having a common culture and dialect and a recognized leader." If we apply the different criteria of this definition to Igbo people we will come up with the following results:

a. Igbo people are not primitive; if we were I would not be offering this distinguished lecture, or would I?;

b. Igbo people are not linked by blood ties, although they may share many cultural traits;

c. Igbo people do not speak one dialect; they speak one language which has scores of major and minor dialects;

d. and as for having one recognized leader, Igbo people would regard the absence of such a recognized leader as the very defining principle of their social and political identity.

Therefore, all in all, Igbo people would score very poorly indeed on the Oxford dictionary test for tribe.

Now, to call them a nation as I now prefer to do is not without problems of its own. (Which reminds me of the little bird that flew off the ground and landed on an anthill, and felt good, not realizing it was still on the ground! I hope my preference of nation over tribe is more substantial than the little bird's illusionary flight.) My little Oxford dictionary defines nation as, "a community of people of mainly common descent, history or language, etc., forming a state or inhabiting a territory." This may not be a perfect fit for the Igbo, but it is close. In addition I like it because, unlike the word tribe, which was given to me, nation is not loaded or derogatory, and there is really no good reason to continue answering a derogatory name simply because somebody has given it to you. The subject of naming, especially naming to put down, will come up in a variety of forms in the course of these deliberations.

The Igbo nation in precolonial times was not quite like any nation most people are familiar with. It did not have the apparatus of centralized government but a conglomeration of hundreds of independent towns and villages each of which shared the running of its affairs among its menfolk according to title, age, occupation, etc.; and its womenfolk who had domestic responsibilities, as well as the management of the scores of four-day and eight-day markets that bound the entire region and its neighbours in a network of daily exchange of goods and news, from far and near.

The town of Ogidi to which my family returned in 1935 was just one of these hundreds of towns which were in reality ministates that cherished their individual identity but also, in a generic way, perceived themselves as Igbo people. Their Igboness would remain a vague identity because it was not called too frequently into use. What mattered to them on a daily basis was the sovereign authority they enjoyed in practical matters in their eight hundred or so villages. As was their habit they made a proverb to sanctify their political attitude: nku di na mba na-eghelu mba nni, every community has enough firewood in its own forests for all the cooking it needs to do.

Competition among these communities has remained a strong feature of Igbo life from antiquity through colonial times to the present. At its worst it could lead to conflict. But there were also compelling reasons for peace and cooperation arising from the need to foster vital regional institutions such as the intricate and vibrant network of markets, the rites and obligations of cross-communal marriages and funerals, the dissemination of recreational songs and dances that one village would travel to learn from another and later, in the role of host and mentor, pass on to a third. Most of these songs and dances were ephemeral and lasted through a couple of seasons. But now and again there were outstanding steps and tunes that stayed a few years. And, once in a long while, perhaps in an entire generation or more, an extraordinary musical sensation would explode through the land. Such an event did occur about the time we returned to Ogidi. It was called Egwu Obi (Song of the Heart) and nicknamed Egwu Tochi (Song of the Torchlight), for Europe was unwrapping her wares of seduction at the threshold. Egwu Obi stayed on for a decade and more while other songs came and went.

Where did they all originate? Rumor had it that they came from a little place called Nzam in the fertile and easygoing flood plain of the Anambra River in the season when the harvests had been gathered in and the floods were back renewing the soil of the farmland. But from whom did the happy people of Nzam learn? Oh, from the birds, of course!

If you should conclude from the emotional quiver in my words that after a rocky start in my hometown I later became rather fond of it, even a little sentimental, you would be entirely right; but I want my reader to remember that my affection did not instantly explode into being at any point I can recall. It began slowly, took its time to grow and develop and ultimately become transformed into a lifelong quest.

In keeping with missionary usage the front room in our house was called the piazza. It was there that my father received his visitors. It was a room with a strange history, as I got to learn later. My father had a younger half-brother whom he had tried in the past, and quite in vain, to convert to Christianity. On account of this failure, perhaps, the relationship between the two tended to be cool. But no matter what, a brother was still a brother, and so when my father had finished building his zinc house his brother had moved in, ostensibly to take care of it for the two or three years my father still had before retirement. But as the Christian owner was far away in the mission field his brother considered it safe to install his heathen shrine of ikenga and other household divinities in the piazza. Perhaps he did not expect my father to be more than mildly disapproving. If so, he was totally mistaken. My father was furious and demanded the immediate removal of the shrine not only from the house but from the compound. Perhaps that was the real cause of the coolness between them. I never did ask my father if he had had the house reconsecrated after my uncle's brief tenancy and desecration, but I seem to recall the vaguest shadow of an indulgent smile on his face as he told the story one more time many years later. Could he have been thinking of the irony of spending his years converting strangers in far-flung parts of Olu and Igbo while Satan in the shape of his half-brother was hard at work in the rear, in the very front room of his own house at home? My father had that kind of gallows humor.

Both my parents were strong and even sometimes uncompromising in their Christian beliefs, but they were not fanatical. Their lives were ruled, I think, as much by reason as by faith; as much by common sense and compassion as by doctrine. My father's half-brother was not the only heathen in our extended family; if anything, he was among a majority. Our home was open to them all, and my father received his peers and relatives— Christian or not—with kola nut and palm-wine in that piazza, just as my mother received her visitors in the parlour. It was from the conversations and disagreements in these rooms, especially the piazza, that I learned much of what I know and have come to value about my history and culture. Many a time what I heard in those days, just hanging around my father and his peers, only became clear to me years and even decades later.

I heard, for example, that one of Ogidi's neighbouring towns had migrated into its present location a long time ago and made a request to Ogidi to settle there. In those days there was plenty of land to go round and Ogidi people welcomed the newcomers, who then made a second and more surprising request—to be shown how to worship the gods of Ogidi. What had they done with their own gods? Ogidi people wondered at first but finally decided that a man who asked you for your god must have a terrible story one should not pry into. So they gave the new people two of Ogidi gods, Udo and Ogwugwu, with one proviso, that the new-comers should not call their newly acquired gods Udo but Udo's son; and not Ogwugwu but Ogwugwu's daughter. Just to avoid any confusion!

For many years this fragment of local lore meant no more to me than one more story of internal migration in Igboland, probably part history and part mythology, the kind of story one might hear invoked or manipulated in a court of law today in boundary litigations between towns. But its profound significance dawned on me later—the reluctance of an Igbo town to foist its religious beliefs and practices on a neighbour across the road, even when it was invited to do so. Surely such a people cannot have had any notion of the psychology of religious imperialism. And that innocence would have placed them at a great disadvantage later when they came to deal with European evangelism. Perhaps the sheer audacity of some stranger wandering thousands of miles from his home to tell them they were worshipping false gods may have left them open-mouthed in amazement—and actually aided their rapid conversion! If so, they were stunned into conversion only, but luckily not all the way to the self-righteousness and zealotry that went with the stranger's audacity. The levelheadedness of my parents would seem to be a result of that good fortune.

It will be useful, I think, to present one or two more examples of the informal education I garnered in my father's front room and other similar settings in my childhood. The first ancestor of Ogidi people was named Ezechuamagha. He was created by Chukwu on the present site of the town. Chukwu then moved a certain distance and planted another primordial man called Ezumaka, father of the neighbouring Nkwele people. For boundary, Chukwu created the Nkisi River to flow between them. Again, just an interesting little piece of folklore. But as I learned more and more about Igbo people, it began to dawn on me that this insistence on separate and individual creations of towns chimed perfectly with their belief that every single human being was a unique creation of chi, Chukwu's agent, assigned exclusively to that individual through his or her life. This chi, this presence of God, in attendance on every human being, is more powerful in the affairs of that person than any local deity or the conspiracy of any number of such deities against that person. I shall return anon to this unprecedented expression of Igbo individuality. But I want us to look first at an analogous proposition about community.

There is a charming little Igbo story which I would have loved to tell you in full but must abbreviate drastically because I have told it elsewhere.

One morning all the animals were going to a meeting to which the town crier had summoned them the night before. Surprisingly the chicken was headed not to the public square like the rest, but away from it. When his neighbours and friends asked him if by any chance he had not heard the summons to the meeting, he said he had indeed heard but, unfortunately, must attend to a very important personal matter that just cropped up. He asked them to convey his good wishes to the assembly and, for good measure, added his declaration to support and abide by its resolutions. The emergency before the animals, as it happened, was the rampant harassment that man had begun to cause them since he learned to offer blood sacrifice to his gods. After a long and heated debate the animals accepted, and passed unanimously, a resolution to offer the chicken to man as his primary sacrificial animal. And it has remained so to this day.

In the worldview of the Igbo the individual is unique; the town is unique. How do they bring the competing claims of these two into some kind of resolution? Their answer is a popular assembly that is small enough for everybody who wishes to be present to do so and to "speak his own mouth," as they like to phrase it.

A people who would make and treasure

that fable of the negligent chicken and the assembly of his fellows must be serious democrats. In all probability they would not wish to live under the rule of kings. The Igbo did not wish to, and made no secret of their disinclination. Sometimes one of them would, believe it or not, actually name his son Ezebuilo: A king is an enemy. I ask you, ladies and gentlemen, to contemplate a society wherein a man might raise his voice in his compound of an afternoon and call out to his son: "A-King-Is-An-Enemy, get me some cold water to drink, will you!"

To assert the worth of the individual by making him not the product of some ongoing, generic creativity but rather of a particular once-and-for-all divine activity is about as far as human imagination can go on the road of uniqueness. To then put this already unprecedented artifact on a piece of land chosen, surveyed and demarcated by God for him may seem like taking matters a trifle far. But we must always remember that the extravagant attire which Metaphor wears to catch our eye is merely a ploy to engage our hearts and minds. It seems to me that the Igbo people, recognizing the primary necessity for individual freedom, as well as the virtual impossibility of its practical realization in society, went out of their way to give the individual a cosmological head start in their creation stories. In this way man might have something approaching a sporting chance in the game of life—an ability to hold his head up and declare, as the Igbo are wont to do, that no man should enter his house through another man's gate.

Similarly, those hundreds of autonomous Igbo villages and towns, so deeply suspicious of political amalgamation, would be stretched to the limit should they ever face an enemy able to wield the resources of a centralized military power, acting directly or through local surrogates. They would need every fortification to be found in their histories and creation myths. The threat of anarchy, always attendant on the Igbo choice of political organization, crept closer and closer to realization as the devastation of the Atlantic Slave Trade reached further and further into their heartland.

The Igbo have always lived in a world of continual struggle, motion and change—a feature conspicuous in the tautness, overreach and torsion of their art; it is like a tightrope walk, a hairbreadth brush with the boundaries of anarchy. This world does not produce easy-going people. Those who visit the Igbo in their home or run into them abroad or in literature are not always prepared for their tense and cocky temperament. The British called them argumentative.

Mister Johnson's Countryman

When my first novel appeared in 1958 with the allusive title *Things Fall Apart*, an offended and highly critical English reviewer in a London Sunday paper titled her piece—cleverly, I must admit—Hurray to Mere Anarchy! But in spite of the cleverness, she could not have known the cosmological fear of anarchy that burdened the characters in my novel, and which W.B. Yeats somehow knew intuitively. In her brightly sarcastic mind, Anarchy, pronounced tongue-in-cheek, could only stand for British imperial rule under attack in some backward corner of the empire by an ungrateful upstart of a native; she did not hear, blending into it, the resonance of an immemorial anxiety. She did not know that metaphor's extravagant attire was donned for good and sober reason.

I have been attempting—with incomplete success I fear—to convey to the reader the quiet education my hometown came slowly to embody for me. I have deliberately left out of account so far the louder, formal education I was receiving simultaneously at school, at Sunday school and in church. As it happened, it was only these foreign aspects of my upbringing that we dignified with the title of education. For us that word was not about Igbo things; it was about faraway places and peoples; and its acquisition was generally painful. Igbo things did not vanish from our lives; they were present but taken for granted, unacknowledged. The atmosphere of the schoolroom was always tense, and you were lucky if a day passed and you did not receive a stroke or two of the teacher's cane. Those who were not very good in schoolwork were, of course, the greatest sufferers. But even I, considered pretty good, still had carried home one day a painful swelling on my head from my albino teacher, which caused my father to walk me right back to school to remonstrate with the teacher, to my alarm and embarrassment.

As the years passed and I got better adjusted to the ways of school, I began to enjoy aspects of its offering, especially reading and English composition. This interest led me in my early teenage, boarding school years to such treasures as *Treasure Island*, *Mutiny on the Bounty*, *Gulliver's Travels*, *Ivanhoe*, *School for Scandal*. My school had a wonderful library and a regulation that forced us to use it. I was not one of those who grumbled about that particular imposition! I was entranced by the faraway and long-ago worlds of the stories, so different from the stories of my home and childhood.

I took a false step at the university; I enrolled to study medicine. But after one academic year of great sadness I switched to the Faculty of Arts. There are half-a-dozen reasons I can give for that episode but I prefer the most patently superstitious. I was abandoning the realm of stories and they would not let me go.

The University College, Ibadan, which had opened its doors in November 1948, was a new experiment in higher education in the closing years of British colonial rule in West Africa. Its syllabus and degrees were closely modelled on, and supervised by, London University. My professors in English were all Europeans from various British and European universities. With one or two exceptions the authors they taught us would have been the same ones they would teach at home: Shakespeare, Milton, Defoe, Swift, Wordsworth,

Coleridge, Keats, Tennyson, Housman, Eliot, Frost, Joyce, Hemingway, Conrad. To this already progressive list they added the Anglo-Irishman, Joyce Cary, whose recent "Nigerian" novel, *Mister Johnson*, had received much critical acclaim in England. America was not to be outdone; *Time* magazine of October 20, 1952, did a cover story on Cary and described *Mister Johnson* as "the best novel ever written about Africa."

The intention of my English professors to introduce us to such an outstanding novel written about a place and people we would be familiar with and therefore easily able to appreciate, was quite unexceptional. But things did not turn out the way they should have. One of my classmates stood up and told an astounded teacher point-blank that the only moment he had enjoyed in the entire book was when the Nigerian hero, Johnson, was shot to death by his British master, Mr. Rudbeck. The rest of us, now astounded too, offered a medley of noises in reaction. My own judgment was that our colleague, and the rest of us perhaps, still had a lot to learn on how to express adverse literary opinion; but beyond that we all shared our colleague's exasperation at this bumbling idiot of a character whom Joyce Cary and our teacher were so assiduously passing off as a poet when he was nothing but an embarrassing nitwit! Now, this incident, as I came to recognize later, was more than just an interesting episode in a colonial classroom. It was a landmark rebellion. Here was a whole class of young Nigerian students, among the brightest of their generation, united in their view of a book of English fiction in complete opposition to their English teacher, who was moreover backed by the authority of metropolitan critical judgment. The issue was not so much who was right as why there was that absolute divide. For it was not my experience that Nigerians, young or old, were much inclined to be unanimous on anything, not even on the greatest issue of the day—the timing of their independence from British rule.

My problem with Joyce Cary's book was

not simply his infuriating principal character, Johnson. More importantly, there is a certain undertow of uncharitableness just below the surface on which his narrative moves and from where, at the slightest chance, a contagion of distaste, hatred and mockery breaks through to poison his tale. Here is a short excerpt from his description of a fairly innocent party given by Johnson to his friends: "the demonic appearance of the naked dancers, grinning, shrieking, scowling, or with faces which seemed entirely dislocated, senseless and unhuman, like twisted bags of lard, or burst bladders." [1] Haven't I encountered this crowd before? Perhaps, in *Heart of Darkness*, in the Congo. But Cary is writing about my home, Nigeria, isn't he?

In the end I began to understand. There is such a thing as absolute power over narrative. Those who secure this privilege for themselves can arrange stories about others pretty much where, and as, they like. Just as in corrupt, totalitarian regimes, those who exercise power over others can do anything. They can bring out crowds of demonstrators whenever they need them. In Nigeria it is called renting a crowd. Has Joyce Cary rented Joseph Conrad's crowd? Never mind. What matters is that Cary has a very strong aversion to the people he is presenting to us. And to the towns and villages where these people live, where the action of his novel takes place:

Fada is the ordinary native town of the Western Sudan. It has no beauty, convenience or health. It is a dwelling-place at one stage from the rabbit warren or the badger burrow; and not so cleanly kept as the latter. It is a pioneer settlement five or six hundred years old, built on its own rubbish heaps, without charm even of antiquity. Its squalor and its stinks are all new. Its oldest compounds, except the Emir's mud box, is not twenty years old. The sun and the rain destroy all its antiquity, even of smell. But neither has it the freshness of the new. All its mud walls are eaten as if by smallpox; half of the mats in any compound are always rotten. Poverty and ignorance, the absolute gov-

ernment of jealous savages, conservative as
only the savage can be, have kept it at the first
frontier of civilization. Its people would not
know the change if time jumped back fifty
thousand years. They live like mice or rats in a
palace floor; all the magnificence and variety
of the arts, the ideas, the learning and the bat-
tles of civilization go on over their heads and
they do not even imagine them.[2]

As everyone knows, sensational writing about
Africa and Africans by European travellers
and others has a long history. Conrad's yelling
crowds were not even his, but a hand-me-
down from earlier times.

Dorothy Hammond and Alta Jablow have
published a study of British writing about
sub-Saharan Africa over a four-hundred-year
period, from the sixteenth century to the
twentieth. They read and analyzed no less than
five hundred volumes of fiction and nonfiction. Their book, titled *The Africa That Never
Was*, shows how a body of fantasy and myth
about Africa developed into a tradition with a

vast storehouse of lurid images to which writers went again and again through the centuries to draw "material" for their books.

An account of the voyage to West Africa in 1561 by the English ship captain John Lok gives us a taste of this writing at the early stages of the tradition. This is what it says about Negroes:

> a people of beastly living, without a God, lawe, religion ... whose women are common for they contract no matrimonie, neither have respect to chastitie ... whose inhabitants dwell in caves and dennes: for these are their houses, and the flesh of serpents their meat as writeth Plinie and Diodorus Siculus. They have no speach, but rather a grinning and chattering. There are also people without heads, having their eyes and mouths in their breasts.[3]

Why did this kind of writing, and variations on it, catch the European imagination and hold it through the centuries into our own day? I could not pursue that question in these lectures without being diverted from my purpose. I will merely say that a tradition does not begin and thrive, as the tradition of British writing about Africa did, unless it serves a certain need. From the moment in the 1560s when the English captain John Hawkins sailed to West Africa and "got into his possession, partly by the sword and partly by other means, to the number of three hundred Negroes,"[4] the European trade in slaves was destined by its very profitability to displace trade in commodities with West Africa. As early as the 1700s British trade in Africa had shifted entirely to slaves. Basil Davidson makes the point that by this time "men in Europe were accustomed to seeing Africans only as men in chains, captives without power, and they transferred their impressions to Africa and the states from which these slaves had come. The belief in African inferiority was already in full bloom."[5]

But the eighteenth century did more than habituate Europeans to the spectacle of Africans "as men in chains," it also presented an abundance of literature tailored to explain or justify that spectacle. Hammond and Jablow have indicated how and where British authors adjusted their writing to suit the times.

> Continuity with earlier writing was maintained … but there was a marked change in the tenor of the literature. Its content shifted from almost indifferent and matter-of-fact reports of what the voyagers had seen to judgmental evaluation of the Africans. … African behavior, institutions and character were not merely disparraged but presented as the negation of all human decencies. … A vested interest in the slave trade produced a literature of devaluation, and since the slave trade was under attack, the most derogatory writing about Africans came from its literary defenders. Dalzel, for instance, prefaced his work with an apologia for slavery: "Whatever evils the slave trade may be attended with … it is mercy … to poor wretches, who … would otherwise suffer from the butcher's knife."[6]

And there, at last, we have it in plain language. The enslavement and expatriation of

Africans was a blessing; and not even a blessing in disguise, but a blessing that is clearly recognizable! A blessing that delivered the poor wretches from a worse fate in their homeland!

The content, style and timing of this literature leave us in no doubt that its production was largely an ancillary service to the slave trade. But on account, no doubt, of its enormous popularity as both sensational entertainment and a salve for the conscience, it also generated a life of its own, so that it did not simply expire when the slave trade was abolished at the beginning of the nineteenth century, but reshaped itself with the tools of trendy scholarly fantasies and pseudo-sciences. In its updated form it stood ready to serve the new historical era of European exploration of Africa and, hot on the heels of that endeavor, colonial occupation itself. Which brings us to the Anglo-Irishman Joyce Cary, who, in the years immediately following the First World War, was serving the British Empire, reluctantly it seems, in a small corner of the territory Britain had recently annexed and named Nigeria and, from some accounts, quite hating the job and, consequently—who knows?—avenging himself by writing a book about it (so devious are the ways of the human psyche!). And at the end of that long and tortuous road (and sentence) we find a class of Nigerian university students in 1952 having to study that book for their Bachelor of Arts degree of London University, and for the first time in their lives having to disagree rather strongly with an English teacher over an English book!

I think I can speak for my classmates if I say that none of us in 1952 knew the heavy historical antecedents of that book. In my secondary school where I had the good fortune of the fine library I have already paid tribute to I did indeed read, on my own, a few "African" novels by such writers as Rider Haggard and John Buchan. But I did not connect the Africa in those riveting adventure stories among savages even remotely with myself or my homeland. Perhaps I was too young. Perhaps I was yet to appropriate Africa from the remote, no man's land of the mind where my first English primer had placed it for me: Once there was a wizard. He lived in Africa. He went to China to get a lamp. Whatever the reason, 1952 was going to be different. And the fact that *Mister Johnson* was not set in some nebulous Africa but claimed to be right there in Nigeria must have helped. My classmates and I could handle the concept of Nigeria with some familiarity and confidence. The time also was right. Just five years down the road, in 1957, our sister colony of the Gold Coast would become the independent state of Ghana and inaugurate the whirlwind decolonization of Africa. So the excitement of change was already in the air in 1952 and, with it, the confidence of heirs to victory over imperial rule. Any white person who did not believe in self-rule for us—and there were quite a number of such people around—was simply called an imperialist. I don't remember us spending sleepless nights analysing such people's motives; they were simply in the nature of things. There was at least one senior professor at Ibadan who had left India at independence in 1947 and fled to us. Such people, facing prospects of a second dethronement, were particularly unamused.

I make this digression merely to point out that eager though we were to get rid of white rule, we did not find it necessary to demonise white people—at least not at that stage. And the reason, I think, is that we were ignorant of the hundreds of years of sustained denigration we and our home had been subjected to in order to make our colonization possible and excusable. If anyone had asked me in 1952 what I thought of Joyce Cary I probably would have been quite satisfied to call him the generic pet name, imperialist!

What his book *Mister Johnson* did for me though was to call into question my childhood assumption of the innocence of stories. It began to dawn on me that although fiction was undoubtedly fictitious it could also be true or false, not with the truth or falsehood of a news item but as to its disinterestedness, its intention, its integrity. Needless to say I did not grasp all of this at one bound but slowly over time through the experience of life and reading. And reading came to mean reading with greater scrutiny and sometimes rereading with adult eyes what I had first read in the innocence of my literary infancy and adolescence.

Saying this the way I have said it may well leave my reader with the impression that I became a sad and disillusioned old man (or "older man" as Americans prefer to say) whose joy in reading has been battered and bruised by the recognition that cruelty can be paraded in many disguises through the avenues of literature by all manner of dubious practitioners. I am glad to reassure everyone about my abiding faith in the profession of literature, and further to suggest that the kind of careful and even cautious mode of reading that I am impliedly advocating does not signal despair; rather it is the strongest vote of confidence we can give our writers and their work—to put them on notice that we will go to their offering for wholesome pleasure and insight, and not for a rehash of old stereotypes which gained currency long ago in the slave trade and poisoned, perhaps forever, the wellsprings of our common humanity. As a writer, I am all for such challenge and such expectations from my readers.

The Empire Fights Back

I will begin this segment with a question: what did I do with my experience of classroom rebellion over *Mister Johnson*? Anyone familiar with the gossip in African literature may have heard that it was that book that made me decide to write. I am not even sure that I have not said it somewhere myself, in one of those occasional seizures of expansive ambition we have to sum up the whole world in a single, neat metaphor. Of course we need such moments now and again to stir things up in our lives. But other times we must be content to stay modest and level-headed, more factual. What *Mister Johnson* did do for me was not to change my course in life and turn me from something else into a writer; I was born that way. But it did open my eyes to the fact that my home was under attack and that my home was not merely a house or a town but, more importantly, an awakening story in whose ambience my own existence had first begun to assemble its fragments into a coherence and meaning; the story I had begun to learn consciously the moment I descended from the lorry that brought me to my father's house in Ogidi, the story that, seventeen years later at the university, I still had only a sketchy, tantalizing knowledge of, and over which even today, decades later, I still do not have sufficient mastery, but about which I can say one thing: that it is not the same story Joyce Cary intended me to have.

For me there are three reasons for becoming a writer. The first is that you have an overpowering urge to tell a story. The second, that you have intimations of a unique story waiting to come out. And the third, which you learn in the process of becoming, is that you consider the whole project worth the considerable trouble—I have sometimes called it terms of imprisonment—you will have to endure to bring it to fruition. For me, those three factors were present, and would have been present had Joyce Cary never been born, or set foot in Nigeria. History, however, had contrived a crossing of our paths, and such crossings may sometimes leave their footmarks, faint or loud, on memory. And if they do, they should be acknowledged.

Another question. Was there any way Joyce Cary could have written a Nigerian novel that we Nigerian students could have accepted as our story? My answer, in retrospect, must be: not likely. And my reason would not be the obvious fact that Cary was a European, but rather because he was the product of a tradition of presenting Africa that he had absorbed at school and Sunday school, in magazines and in British society in general, at the end of the nineteenth century. In theory, a good writer might outgrow these influences, but Cary did not.

In their Introduction to *The Africa That Never Was*, Hammond and Jablow tell us that the large number of writers they studied "were not, and could not be, selected for literary merit" and that there were many more "bad" writers than "good" ones in their sample. (Which, I dare say, is hardly surprising.) They then identify Conrad, Cary, Greene and Huxley (not Aldous but Elspeth) among the better writers (which is still OK by me—it only tells us how bad the bad ones must be). But when they proceed to praise these four for their handling of Africa in their books, I don't quite know what to make of it:

> The better writers, such as Conrad, Cary, Greene and Huxley ... use the conventions of the tradition with skill and subtlety. Each of them has an unmistakably individual style in which he or she selectively exploits the conventions, without allowing the writing to become overwhelmed by them. They all have

more to say about Africa than the merely conventional clichés, along with the talent to say it well.[7]

I suppose we can all differ as to the exact point where good writing becomes overwhelmed by racial cliché. But overwhelmed or merely undermined, literature is always badly served when an author's artistic insight yields place to stereotype and malice. And it becomes doubly offensive when such a work is arrogantly proffered to you as your story. Some people may wonder if, perhaps, we were not too touchy, if we were not oversensitive. We really were not. And I have a somewhat unusual reason for saying so.

Although my classmates and I would not have known it at the time, the London publishing house of Methuen had brought out the year before, in 1951, a little book titled simply *West Africa*. Its author, F. J. Pedler, was a highly respected public servant in Britain, with considerable experience of West Africa. Although the book was not entirely free of the stereotypes of contemporary British colonial writing, it was in some ways remarkably advanced for its time, and even for today. One small example will suffice. "It is misleading," Mr. Pedler wrote, "when Europeans talk of Africans buying a wife."[8] Although he did not mention Joyce Cary by name it is inconceivable that he would not have been aware of him or of his much celebrated novel *Mister Johnson*, in which that very stereotype was exploited for all it was worth in the episode in which Johnson, after much haggling, buys himself a local girl, Bamu, as wife.

But what I find truly remarkable about Pedler's book is the prominence he gave to, and the faith he had in, African literature that was not even in existence yet: "A country's novels reveal its social condition. West Africa has no full-length novels, but a few short stories may serve the purpose. We quote from two recent publications which show how educated West Africans themselves describe some of the features of social life in their own country." Pedler then proceeded to summarize for his reader two short stories published in a magazine in 1945 in the British colony of the Gold Coast. He devoted almost three pages of his short book to this matter and then concluded as follows: "Here is a dramatic treatment of a contemporary social phenomenon which leaves one with the hope that more West Africans may enter the field of authorship and give us authentic stories of the lives of their own people."[9]

These brief quotations speak volumes to us on the issue of peoples and their stories. We should note Pedler's phrases: West Africans themselves; their own country; authentic stories; of their own people. Without calling any names this extraordinary Englishman seemed to be engaged in a running argument against an age-old practice: the colonization of one people's story by another. In sidestepping Joyce Cary and all the other high-profile practitioners of this brand of writing and going, in search of authenticity, to two unpretentious short stories written by two completely unknown West African authors whose names did not ring any bell at all, Pedler was putting himself decisively and prophetically on the side of the right of a people to take back their own narrative. And because he was British, and because we, the students at Ibadan, did not even know of him, nor he presumably of us, our little rebellion in class one year after his book can, in retrospect, assume the status of a genuine, disinterested service to literature, and transcend the troubling impression it might otherwise easily create, of a white/black, British/Nigerian divide.

Incidentally, Pedler's prayer for West African novels was instantly answered. There was already in the works, as we now know, a startling literary concoction from the pen of a Nigerian coppersmith, Amos Tutuola, which Faber would publish in 1952. It may not have been the social realism which F. J. Pedler had presumably hoped for but an odyssey in peculiar English, which roamed about from realism to magic and back again, as in old Africa. But no matter, *The Palm-Wine Drinkard* opened the floodgates to modern West African writing. Hot on its heels came another Nigerian, Cyprian Ekwensi, with *People of the City*; Camara Laye of Guinea with *L'Enfant Noir*; my *Things Fall Apart*; Mongo Beti of Cameroon and his countryman, Ferdinand Oyono, with *Poor Christ of Bomba* and *Houseboy*, respectively; Cheikh Hamidou Kane of Senegal with *Ambiguous Adventure*.

Looking back now on that incredible 1950s decade and all the intersecting events I have been describing, each of which seemed at first sight to be about its own separate little errand but then chanced upon these others on a large, open space such as is used to hold a big market once in eight days and abandoned again to a profound and watchful emptiness till another market-day—looking back on all this, it does become easy to indulge a temptation to see History as mindful, purposeful; and to see the design behind this particular summons and rendezvous as the signal at long last to end Europe's imposition of a derogatory narrative upon Africa, a narrative designed to call African humanity into question.

As we have seen, Captain John Lok's voyage to West Africa in 1561 provided an early model of what would become a powerful and enduring tradition. One of his men had described the Negroes as "a people of beastly living, without a God, laws, religion."[10] Three hundred and fifty years later we find that this model, like the Energizer Bunny, is still running strong, beating away on its tin drum. "Unhuman" was how Joyce Cary, in the early part of our own century, saw his African dancers. One generation before him, Joseph Conrad had created a memorable actor/narrator who could be greatly troubled by the mere thought of his Africans being human, like himself: "Well, you know, that was the worst of it—this suspicion of their not being inhuman."[11]

A more deadly deployment of a mere sixteen words it would be hard to imagine. I think it merits close reading. Note first the narrator's suspicion; just suspicion, nothing more. And note also that even the faint glimmer of apparent charitableness around this speculation is not, as you might have thought, a good thing, but actually the worst of it! And note finally, the coup de grâce of double negation, like a pair of prison guards, restraining that problematic being on each side.

Hammond and Jablow tell us that African characters in all the fiction they studied are invariably "limited to a few stock figures [and] are never completely human."[12] And the quite reasonable conclusion they drew from this was that the writers of this fiction had presumably come to see their contrived portrayal as "the only way to write about Africa."[13]

Four hundred years was indeed a very long time; and the hundreds and hundreds of books churned out in Britain, Europe and elsewhere to create the tradition of an Africa inhabited by barely recognizable humanity have taken their toll. But could it hold sway for all time as "the only way to write about Africa"? Of course not. Why? Because abuse is not sanctified by its duration or abundance; it must remain susceptible to question and challenge, no matter how long it takes. The nemesis for this particular abuse came in our time, and we are all lucky for that privilege.

Since I have used the research findings of Dorothy Hammond and Alta Jablow to support my argument in this segment of my presentation I might as well conclude it in their actual words:

> The literary tradition that developed over four centuries of British-African contact has now finally become attenuated. Few British are writing about Africa. The Empire is gone and the British population in Africa with it. Africa is no longer the "great unknown" waiting to be discovered. It has become just another post-colonial area where the indigenous people must live and deal with the vicissitudes of life. ... Most of the significant writing about Africa is now being done by African writers such as Amos Tutuola, Chinua Achebe, Wole Soyinka and others.[14]

I like being on that short list, but I must tell you it is very short, almost bizarre in its truncation. Those "others" left out are legion.

Everywhere new ways to write about Africa have appeared, reinvesting the continent and its people with humanity, free at last of those stock situations and stock characters, "never completely human," that had dominated European writing about Africa for hundreds of years. The new literature that erupted so dramatically and so abundantly in the 1950s and 1960s showed great variety in subject matter, in style of presentation and, let's face it, in levels of skill and accomplishment. But there was one common thread running through it all: the thread of a shared humanity linking the author to the world of his creation; a sense that even in the most tempting moments of grave disappointment with this world, the author remains painfully aware that he is of the same flesh and blood, the same humanity as its human inhabitants.

This new literature of Africa took almost everyone by surprise and elicited an impres-

sive range of responses in different people and
different places. From their own account
of events the British publishing house of
William Heinemann, who brought out my
first novel in 1958, were not exactly waiting
for it when it arrived in their editorial offices.
Having coped with nothing quite like it before, they didn't at first know, for a start, where
to send it for a reader's comment; and when
the reader they finally chose turned in an un-
usually strong recommendation couched in
one brief sentence of seven words, they still
hedged their bet by ordering a very small
print run of two thousand copies. Fortunately
for me (and for them) one of their directors,
Alan Hill, was an adventurer with all the right
instincts. He was able to persuade his colleagues on the board to gamble further and issue a paperback edition of the novel, and with
it to launch an unprecedented program of
publications to be called the African Writers
Series. I had by this time obliged them with
my second novel, and Alan Hill's daring sortie
into African publishing was founded on the

still rather slender promise of four books—my two novels, a novel by another Nigerian, Cyprian Ekwensi, and Kenneth Kaunda's autobiography, *Zambia Shall Be Free*.

The launching of Heinemann's African Writers Series was like the umpire's signal for which African writers had been waiting on the starting line. In one short generation an immense library of new writing had sprung into being from all over the continent and, for the first time in history, Africa's future generations of readers and writers—youngsters in schools and colleges—began to read not only *David Copperfield* and other English classics that I and my generation had read but also works by their own writers about their own people. The excitement generated by this largely unexpected event was very great indeed and continues to delight many people to this day, in Africa and beyond. The British poet and broadcaster Edward Blishen said of the African Writers Series, "I saw a whole new potentially great world literature come into being."[15]

And as for Alan Hill, his venture into African publishing had become an instant success story. It established Heinemann as a powerful force in British and Commonwealth publishing. And it was also a great business success for Heinemann, which showed its appreciation by putting Mr. Hill at the head of its entire operation. In 1980 his services were recognized by Queen Elizabeth II herself with the royal accolade of Commander of the British Empire, albeit at a time when there was no empire left to command, as another Britisher put it.

The story of Alan Hill and Heinemann helps to illustrate the diversity of responses by outsiders to the emergence and significance of modern African literature in the middle of the twentieth century; for we must remember that Heinemann was by no means the first British publisher to set foot on African soil. There was already a small number of such publishers doing business in different British colonies, selling such books as the Bible and other devotional literature, as well as school textbooks, written by British authors and produced in Britain. In the course of colonial evolution these earlier publishers had slowly begun to take the African consumer into account in a minimalist process culminating, in my own schooldays, in simplified readers written in "basic" English for the likes of me. That was how I came to read those immortal words: "Once there was a wizard. He lived in Africa. He went to China to get a lamp." Anyone who underrates the publisher's effort to address my special needs as an African child in that passage has not seen what my older siblings had read, a few years before me! These gradual changes in the edges of our education continued until Jack and Jill who went down the hill were given brown faces. Which was roughly the frontier of publishing innovation when Alan Hill came on the scene looking not for a warehouse in which to off-load his British books but for African writers. And his quest was so successful that other publishers saw the light and joined in, and the face of publishing in Africa was changed for good.

And it was truly a case of one publisher deciding to make a difference.

I must now touch upon a corresponding variety in individual responses by readers, critics and fellow writers from outside Africa. But I must do it gingerly and with brevity for fear of arousing the faintest suspicion of wishing to prescribe the kind of response we should get. Having claimed and exercised the freedom to tell my own story, I recognize that I must stand ready for the full range of others' responses, be they favorable or unfavorable, well-informed or not. And even learn from them!

Perhaps it would be appropriate to shift the focus here away from myself to Amos Tutuola, that "sensational literary freak" as some called him, whose first novel, *The Palm-Wine Drinkard*, published by the prestigious house of Faber in London in 1952, had led the way for modern West African literature in English.

The celebrated Welsh poet Dylan Thomas recognized Tutuola's merit instantly and sang him a paean by way of a review captioned "Blithe Spirits" in the *Sunday Observer*. It was a brief essay but Thomas wasted no time and seemingly no effort getting right into the spirit of Tutuola's tale. He also captured the letter of it and gave a masterful, and joyous, summary of the plot such as no one, to my knowledge, has ever bettered, for its comprehensiveness, accuracy or humor. Although short as reviews go it is still too long, alas, to quote here. So I will, regretfully, dismember it and cite only a fragment, the final paragraph:

> The writing is nearly always terse and direct, strong, wry, flat and savoury; the big and often comic, terrors are as near and understandable as the numerous small details of price, size and number; and nothing is too prodigious or too trivial to put down in this tall, devilish story.[16]

As far as I know Dylan Thomas never went to Africa; his recognition of Tutuola's merit could not, therefore, have come from specialist knowledge of Tutuola's background and culture. I think it was rather the spontaneous recognition and acknowledgement of one blithe spirit by another, like the esoteric salutation given by one ancestral mask to its fellow in Igbo masquerade.

Now let us consider the response of another British author, Elspeth Huxley, to the same novel. In a sweeping, magisterial book of nonfiction published in 1954 Huxley passed the following judgment on Tutuola and, while at it, took a swipe at African art in general:

> *The Palm-Wine Drinkard* is a folk tale, full of the queer, distorted poetry, the deep and dreadful fears, the cruelty, the obsession with death and spirits, the macabre humour, the grotesque imagery of the African mind.
>
> African art, if it is genuine, is never comfortable, noble or serene; perhaps for that reason it may never reach the heights—rather will it explore the depths of fear, torment and intimidation, with a relish of humour. It is possessed by spirits and the spirits are malign.[17]

Unlike Dylan Thomas, Elspeth Huxley did have direct, personal experience of Africa, and wrote much fiction and nonfiction about the continent and its people. She probably even considered herself an African, like so many other white settlers in the fertile, comfortable highlands the British had taken away from the Gikuyu in Kenya. Indeed Mrs. Huxley was often called the spokesman for the white settler community. So profound was her expertise about the natives also that she could tell their smells apart. In one of her books, *The Flame Trees of Thika*, she says she liked the vegetarian smell of the Gikuyu, "dry, peppery, yet rich and deep." Although it nauseated some Europeans, she tells us, she, for one, grew to enjoy it. As for the tribes from the Victoria Nyanza basin who were, she says, meat-eaters, "and sometimes cannibals," Huxley did not care for their "much stronger and more musky, almost acrid smell."[18]

Enough said, I think, for now. A more interesting, more astonishing response to Tutuola's book came from some of his own people living in England. In 1954 a minor war broke out in the pages of *West Africa*, a biweekly journal published in London, over Amos Tutuola who had just published his second novel, *My Life in the Bush of Ghosts*. A number of Nigerian students in Britain began to write to the editor questioning the good faith of the British and the French and the Americans who were making all that to-do about a couple of books of folk tale written in bad English. One of the writers confessed he had "unfortunately (or perhaps fortunately)" not read either book, but was convinced from what he could gather about them that they had no literary value whatsoever. He was certain that Tutuola was in it just for the money, and his European admirers for the opportunity he had provided them to "confirm their concepts of Africa."[19] Fortunately there was one letter-writer who disagreed strongly with the others. And who, mercifully, had also read Tutuola's two books!

Looking back across four decades to these early responses to the emergence of modern

African literature one must feel unconditional satisfaction that the literature happened at all but also a little anxious about what remains to be done, in Africa and in the world at large, for it seems clear to me that the central questions of dispossession and its consequences are not matters for Africa alone to worry about.

Stories at War

The outburst of European activity across the earth and over the oceans in the period we call the Age of Discovery brought Europe in one bound to the doorstep of Africa, with some dire results for African societies, chief among them the Atlantic slave trade and colonial occupation.

Man is a story-making animal. He rarely passes up an opportunity to accompany his works and his experiences with matching stories. The heavy task of dispossessing others calls for such a story and, of course, its makers: oral historians or griots in the past; mere writers today. Repossession, if and when it does occur, needs also its enabling stories and the singers and writers to compose them. But as we can all appreciate, there will be a wide gulf of difference between the story put out by the first group to explain or camouflage their doings and the reconstitutive annals made up by those who will struggle to reclaim their history.

Let us imagine that someone has come along to take my land from me. We would not expect him to say he is doing it because of his greed, or because he is stronger than I. Such a confession would brand him as a scoundrel and a bully. So he hires a story-teller with a lot of imagination to make up a more appropriate story which might say, for example, that the land in question could not be mine because I had shown no aptitude to cultivate it properly for maximum productivity and profitability. It might go on to say that the reason for my inefficiency is my very low I.Q. and explain that my brain had stopped growing at the age of ten.

Anyone who thinks this is a joke has not read Elspeth Huxley's African books. Here is a sample from *White Man's Country*, one of her non-fiction works:

> perhaps it may be, as some doctors have suggested, that his brain is different: that it has a shorter growing period and possesses less well-formed, less cunningly arranged cells than that of the Europeans—in other words, that there is a fundamental disparity between the capabilities of his brain and ours.[20]

These opinions were not invented by Huxley. She took them ready-made out of well-worn European folklore about Africa to support her case that Kenya indeed belonged to the white man and that the resident English peer, Lord Delamere, was indisputably its founder. As if this proposition was not surreal enough, Huxley added a strange new element to it: "This country had belonged neither to the black man nor the white, but to the wild animals, and now they were being dispossessed."[21] Was this another way of saying: OK, if I'm not to have it, I'll make sure the blacks don't?

Mrs. Huxley, the griot for white settlers, had done her best for her kinsmen. But as we have seen, the leader of that tribe was a certain nobleman, Lord Delamere, who had gone from his estate in England on a hunting safari to Kenya in Africa, found that he rather liked the place and decided to stay. The British colonial administration that was entrenching itself there was pleased with the august visitor's decision and awarded him 100,000 acres of prime land it had appropriated when Britain had declared Kenya a crown colony in 1902. Lord Delamere was soon organising the white farmers of Kenya and its adjoining territories to oppose any recognition of the rights of the Africans to the land or their participation in any political activity in the colony. His uncompromising stance began to lead him more and more into opposition even to the government in London. Such was the heroic material available to

Mrs. Huxley in her creative enterprise; and she did what she could with what zeal she could muster. But perhaps even she had her visitations of doubt.

I like to think that the title of her next book, *On the Edge of the Rift*, was either a conscious admission of the precariousness of her proprietorial perch; or, more interestingly still, a piece of—shall we say—unconscious Freudian irony! But I may be underrating altogether the power of tribal advocacy.

Needless to say, the Kenyans themselves had a completely different story to tell, a story founded on a mystical, immemorial relationship between them and the red earth of their homeland. About the time Huxley was publishing *White Man's Country*, a young African nationalist, Jomo Kenyatta, whose varied experiences at that point had included menial service in Kenya as houseboy and cook to a white settler, and student in London of the celebrated anthropologist, Bronislaw Malinowski, was preparing for publication a thesis on his Gikuyu people, at

the famous London School of Economics
and Political Science. His title, *Facing Mount
Kenya*, suggested a devotional positioning, a
taking of bearings. It is interesting and, I
think, significant that Jomo Kenyatta chose to
include in his study of his people a short
piece of fiction, a fable and political satire,
which he called "The Gentlemen of the Jungle," to illustrate, in his own words, "the relationship between the Gikuyu and the
Europeans."[22] It is the story of a dispossession
that began with a little act of hospitality by
the dispossessed. A man in his hut allows his
friend, the elephant, to put his trunk into the
hut, out of the rain. The elephant, in stages
and against the man's protests, eases the rest of
him into the small hut and finally forces the
man outside. The resulting commotion
brings King Lion himself to the scene. He
immediately appoints a royal commission of
inquiry to look into the man's complaint. But
the commission is made up of the Rt. Hon.
Mr. Elephant's cabinet colleagues, like Mr.
Rhinoceros, Mr. Buffalo, and the Rt. Hon.

Mr. Fox as chairman. The commission met and heard evidence from the elephant and from such witnesses as Mr. Hyena; but they cut short the man's testimony because, they said, he had not confined himself to relevant facts. Before passing their judgment they first retired to have a feast prepared by Mrs. Elephant. Their ruling was that unoccupied space existed in the man's hut and was legitimately put into use by the elephant whose action was ultimately good for the man himself. They also gave the man permission to look for another site and build another hut more suited to his needs. Afraid to antagonise his powerful neighbours the man accepted their ruling.

The next hut he built was immediately appropriated by Mr. Rhinoceros, and another inquiry was conducted by another royal commission. And so it continued until all the lords of the jungle had been accommodated in huts the man built for himself.

Convinced at long last that he could expect no justice from the animals and their royal commission, the man decided to take matters in his own hands. He said: Ng'enda thi ndagaga motegi, which we are told "literally means: there is nothing that treads the earth that cannot be trapped, or in other words, you can fool people for a time, but not forever."[23]

Something ominous is happening here. First we encounter a secret thought wrapped in a language we are not supposed to understand, and then we are told it means two quite different things. We begin to sense trouble in the air, the end of narrative openness and trust.

The man set to work and built the grandest hut of all; and no sooner was it done than the rulers of the jungle each rushed from his old hut to occupy the new one. And soon they were fighting, "and while they were all embroiled together the man set the hut on fire and burnt it to the ground, jungle lords and all. Then he went home, saying: 'Peace is costly, but it's worth the expense,' and lived happily ever after."[24] Kenyatta's story reads like a prophecy of the Kenya struggle for liberation, of the bitter armed rebellion the British called Mau Mau, the concessions they began to make thereafter, leading to independence under Jomo Kenyatta as Prime Minister in 1963. The statue of Lord Delamere in the center of Nairobi was pulled down and Jomo Kenyatta took his place. Kenya has not exactly lived happily ever after, but that's another story. "The Gentlemen of the Jungle" with its ever-ready royal commission of inquiry can be read today as a hilarious fable, as an indulgent parody of British imperial practices. Sixty years ago when it was first published it must have looked like a subversive and seditious document. Mrs. Huxley would not have been amused. Certainly she went ahead, many years later, to hand over the land of Kenya to the animals!

I have given more space to Elspeth Huxley in these remarks than she might otherwise get in Africa's contemporary literary and political scheme of things. But I consider her very important indeed for what she reveals to us of

the rarely considered consequences of the act
of dispossession on those who carry it out or
offer their services in defence of it. The emi-
nent British colonial historian Dame Margery
Perham praised Huxley's *White Man's Country*
as "the best apologia for white settlement that
has been written"[25]; and Lord Lugard, emi-
nent builder of the British Empire in Africa
admired "her exceptional knowledge of African life."[26] With such high credentials how
could Mrs. Huxley miss so completely the
significance of Tutuola's pioneering novel *The
Palm-Wine Drinkard*, dismissing it with a wave
of the hand as "the grotesque imagery of the
African mind," and with it African art in general as possessed by malign spirits? Was it a
simple failure of insight or a willful denial and
repudiation of what stood before her eyes?
Huxley's choice of words does suggest the latter to me. And if so she would not have lacked
a motive. She was engaged in spinning stories
to validate the transfer of African lands to
white settlers. To put it rather brutally, she was
engaged in forging fake title deeds. And be-

cause she was a bright and, at heart, a decent human being, she was uncomfortable whenever the rightful owner came in sight; hence her jumpy and grumpy review of Tutuola. It comes with playing fast and loose with the facts.

Dylan Thomas was a free spirit. He did not require, and did not wait for, an invitation to enter into the spirit of an African homecoming celebration. He had freed himself, as Huxley had not, from the legacy of guilt from acts of dispossession in past centuries, nor had he enlisted, as she had, in the service of new forms of dispossession that sustained the presence and the lavish lifestyle of white settlers in places like Kenya. And the price to be paid by all who live in such places is to live with fear and hostility. But for an artist there is additional penalty to take home—a narrowness, a blunting of integrity, of the faculty of creative response to all the world. For as Dylan Thomas himself wrote in 1953, "There is only one position for an artist anywhere; and that is, upright."[27]

But unfortunate though it may be, the penalty an artist suffers for embracing a narrowness of vision can hardly be called unjustified. What is both unfortunate and unjust is the pain the person dispossessed is forced to bear in the act of dispossession itself and subsequently in the trauma of a diminished existence. The range of aberrations and abnormalities fostered by this existence can be truly astounding. Take, for instance, those straitlaced Nigerian students in London in 1952 who felt so ashamed and embarrassed by Tutuola's story of their homeland, written, as they saw it, in incorrect English, that some of them went up in arms without reading the book! Their nervous confusion, the fragility of their awareness and self-esteem can only be imagined. Wasn't it part of that syndrome which told us while I was growing up that it was more civilized to fetch water in gallon tins from Europe than with clay pots made by ourselves? And, as we speak, have we grown wiser and put all that foolishness aside? Here is what a much advertised author living in London said in 1986 about her fellow writers toiling away in Nigeria:

> Writing coming from Nigeria, from Africa (I know this because my son does the criticism) sounds quite stilted. After reading the first page you tell yourself you are plodding. But when you are reading the same thing written by an English person or somebody who lives here you find you are enjoying it because the language is so academic, so perfect. Even if you remove the cover you can always say who is an African writer. But with some of my books you can't tell that easily any more because, I think, using the language every day and staying in the culture my Africanness is, in a way, being diluted. My paperback publisher, Collins, has now stopped putting my books in the African section.[28]

That does it for all those beleaguered African writers struggling at home to tell the story of their land. They should one and all emigrate to London or Paris to dilute their Africanness and become, oh, "so academic, so perfect."

The psychology of the dispossessed can be truly frightening.

Today,
the Balance of Stories

Thinking of an appropriate metaphor to celebrate the beginning of the reclamation of the African story, I was initially drawn to a proverb about lions that had come my way in the fairly recent past. An American researcher had apparently encountered the proverb in his work and was wondering if I might tell him where it came from. It went like this: Until the lions produce their own historian, the story of the hunt will glorify only the hunter. Unfortunately, I couldn't help the researcher with what he wanted to know, even though I did my best to help. A friend I telephoned in Nairobi, Kenya, just chuckled and said vaguely that "it sounded like the Masai," and left it there. Which led me to a recognition of something I hadn't quite considered before—that those who inhabit the world of proverbs do not spend sleepless nights worrying over provenance. They know a good proverb when they hear it and simply add it to their stock.

On a number of occasions since the researcher told me that proverb I have profited by its use, and it has never failed to light up an audience for me or enliven a discourse. But in a rather strange way, I also recognized fairly quickly that there was something about it that did not fully agree with my deepest intent. In the end, I realized what the problem was: the lion himself. The lion projects too strong an aura of strength to be entirely satisfactory to me as a messenger of truth. I discovered that I did not really want to see the score of narratives between me and my detractor settled by recourse to power, other than the innate power of stories themselves. And I recognized that this choice of weapons was determined for me not by logic or philosophy but by mere temperament. And this issue of temperament ties in with the fact, for example, that I have never held a gun in my life—a fact so shameful, I dare say, at the age of sixty-eight as to call for some kind of apology. And I would make one now if I didn't think that one apology might trigger the need for others even more consequential; for example what about an apology for the somewhat autobiographical and anecdotal mode of these presentations to which a totally reasonable person might well have come with more severe, more rigorous expectations? So it is best to leave apologies severely alone. And proceed to forgo, with residual regret, the high drama of the lion-historian for the rather pedestrian metaphor of the British post office. For this alternative I am indebted, by the way, to Salman Rushdie, who, I believe, was the first writer to describe the phenomenon of postcolonial literature in four memorable words: The Empire Writes Back. The very idea of presenting all that sensational writing from the metropolis and the angry, bitter response it provoked in the fullness of time among the natives in the provinces as a mere exchange of correspondence is a truly appealing miracle of sublimation. I witnessed, as a child, the incorporation of my village into the vast network of postal services that knit the British Empire together, without, of course, understanding what I was seeing. A small, one-room house with a huge front window that came down in the morning to serve as a counter had been put up in the Native Court premises on the great highway that cut our village in two. A tall, young man in his penultimate year in the primary school was hired as a postal agent, although we all came to call him by the more impressive title of postmaster or P. M. Another villager who was just literate enough to decipher names and addresses on envelopes was hired as postman and given a khaki uniform and a bicycle. Our town's participation in a network of imperial transactions was made manifest in the daily coming and going at our post office. Other postmen came from surrounding towns and villages, bringing letters in canvas bags secured with brass rings and locks, and taking away other bags. But the real event of the day was the majestic arrival of the six-wheeled, blue-painted lorry with the name Royal Mail emblazoned in big, yellow letters on its brow and on each flank. It brought in and took away many more bags and bundles of letters and other papers than all the bicycles together. We, the children, had a special name for it, which we called out with that mixture of admiration and fear children can handle so well: Ogbu-akwu-ugwo, which means Killer-that-doesn't-pay-back, a rather strong name, you might say, for a truck that merely wanted to deliver the king's mail! But strong language is in the very nature of the dialogue between dispossession and its rebuttal. The two sides never see the world in the same light. Thus, the British might boast that they had the first empire in history on which the sun never set; to which an Indian would reply: Yes, because God cannot trust an Englishman in the dark!

And so the little post office in my village, which the British, no doubt, considered an agent of their most excellent Pax Britannica, was seen by its immediate beneficiaries as a killer who will not be called to account; in other words, a representative of anarchy in the world.

Although it was children I remember calling the Royal Mail by its terrible alias, I am pretty certain that the adults were responsible for creating it and letting it loose among us, ostensibly for our education in road safety!

In the war between dispossession and its nemesis civilization itself regresses into barbarism; words become weapons again rather than tools; ploughshares are beaten back into spears. Fear and suspicion take over from openness and straight conversation, as we saw happen, between the Man and the animals in Jomo Kenyatta's "The Gentlemen of the Jungle," with such dire consequences.

The time has come round to a change of millennia when, history tells us, all kinds of excitable people are apt to go bonkers; when even more equable souls like ourselves may get high on prophecies. The last time around W.E.B. Du Bois had held high hopes for the twentieth century on the matter of race. Mindful of that, alas, unfinished business, my hope for the twenty-first is that it will see the first fruits of the balance of stories among the world's peoples. The twentieth century for all its many faults did witness a significant beginning, in Africa and elsewhere in the so-called Third World, of the process of "re-storying" peoples who had been knocked silent by the trauma of all kinds of dispossession. I was lucky to be present at one theater of that reclamation. And I know that such a tremendously potent and complex human reinvention of self—calling, as it must do, on every faculty of mind and soul and spirit; drawing as it must, from every resource of memory and imagination and from a familiarity with our history, our arts and culture; but also from an unflinching consciousness of the flaws that blemished our inheritance—such an enterprise could not be expected to be easy. And it has not been.

The ferocity occasioned by the act of dispossession and its continuing aftermath of cultural loss and confusion can usher in a "season of anomy" as Wole Soyinka aptly calls it in the title of a novel. Nadine Gordimer, whose fate was to witness the hideously candid South African arena of this struggle, opens her remarkable, short novel *July's People* with an epigraph from Antonio Gramsci's *Prison Notebooks*: "The old is dying and the new cannot be born; in this interregnum there arises a great diversity of morbid symptoms." The Zimbabwean writer Tsitsi Dangarembga took the title of her first novel, *Nervous Conditions*, from Fanon's social-psychiatric analysis of the colonized native.

There are many more examples from past, recent and ongoing writing to show that we are not complacent about the risks and dangers that might attend the business of reclamation. We recognize these dangers in our own lives, in our friends and societies and in the imaginary world of our works. Let us think back for one moment to those nervous Nigerian students in London in the 1950s who were so embarrassed by the novel *The Palm-Wine Drinkard*. Were they really responding to the book? We have to answer no because some of them had not even read it. Perhaps they were not so much responding to anything external as from something deep inside of them—a badly damaged sense of self.

And then, thirty years later, we have the good Nigerian lady, also in London, who actually writes novels—a huge step forward, except that she seems to make every effort to minimize her "Africanness" so that her books can pass in British bookstores!

An erosion of self-esteem is one of the commonest symptoms of dispossession. It does not occur only at the naïve level such as we have just alluded to; even more troubling is when it comes in the company of sophistication and learning. It may then take the form of an excessive eagerness to demonstrate flair and worldliness; a facility to tag on to whatever the metropolis says is the latest movement, without asking the commonsense question: later than what? Let us imagine a man who stumbles into an alien ritual in its closing stages when the devotees are winding down to a concluding chorus of amens, and who immediately and enthusiastically takes up the singing with such loudness and gusto that the owners of the ritual stop their singing and turn, one and all, to look in wonder at this postmodernist stranger. Their wonder increases tenfold when they ask the visitor later what kind of modernism his people had had, and it transpires that neither he nor his people had ever heard the word modernism.

I do not believe that the balance of stories, which I speak and dream of and would wish more than anything else on the twenty-first century, will be facilitated by the eccentricities of that postmodernist stranger. Which, I hasten to add, is not to say that I would have somebody pronounce a fatwa on him or his works. As a matter of fact eccentricities such as his can liven up the gathering and may even save it from righteousness and solemnity; but in the final reckoning the people who will advance the universal conversation will be not copycats but those able to bring hitherto untold stories, along with new ways of telling.

After a short period of dormancy and a little self-doubt about its erstwhile imperial mission, the West may be ready to resume its old domineering monologue in the world. Certainly there is no lack of zealots urging it to do so. They call it "taking a hard look" at things. The result is a hardening of views on such issues as the African slave trade and the European colonization of Africa, with the result, generally, of absolving Europe from much of the blame and placing it squarely on African shoulders.

This turn of events should not surprise us. Despite the significant changes that have taken place in the last four or five decades, the wound of the centuries is still a long way from healing. And I believe that the curative power of stories can move the process forward.

Which is why one tends to be rather impatient with one's colleagues, from Africa and other dispossessed places, who don't seem to know the score. Or, worse, who do but choose the fleshpots.

On April 1, 1991, *Forbes* magazine carried a startling editorial entitled "Shakespeare, Plato and other racist pigs." It turned out to be an indictment on "many academics in American universities" accused by the editorial of "deliberately trying to turn their students against traditional Western values" and of "disguising their activities as an effort to understand other cultures." How, it went on, does one respond to these "academics and scribblers who blame Western culture for all the world's ills, real and imagined?" Without actually saying "Hurray" but evidently suggesting it the editorial goes on: "Along comes Sir Vidiadhar S. Naipaul, one of the greatest living writers in English." And the day was saved. Sir Vidia single-handedly trounced the ragtag army of un-American activists hiding in the academy! Perhaps I should have told you before now that a small, full-length photo of Naipaul leaning nonchalantly on a solid stone wall occupied the right hand corner of the double-column editorial. And also that on the opposite page was a 1907 Rolls Royce Silver Ghost, still going strong, according to the commercial.

I think the proximity of the priceless Rolls Royce coupé to the celebrated writer must be merely coincidental but also, in a funny kind of way, quite appropriate.

The occasion for celebrating Naipaul in the *Forbes* magazine editorial was his Walter Wriston lecture "Our Universal Civilization" at the Manhattan Institute. Naipaul's thesis in his lecture was that the civilization that began in Europe and spread to America has earned the right to be accepted as the civilization for everyone because it has made "extraordinary attempt to accommodate the rest of the world, and all the currents of that world's thought." No wonder *Forbes* magazine was so ecstatic!

Naipaul's participation in what he calls the universal civilization had been known by his readers long before his Manhattan Institute lecture. He had travelled to troubled parts of the world and written scathing accounts about them. The poverty in India, his ancestral home, filled him with disgust, and his reaction brought him into conflict with many Indians who were not necessarily defensive but still found his attitude too insensitive, arrogant and plain ignorant. In a review in the *New Republic* of June 10, 1991, Akeel Bilgrami wrote: "His cultural commentary typically combined an effortless contempt with a cultivated ignorance of the historical and the institutional sources of a culture's surface presentation." But it was perhaps in his African novel *A Bend in the River* that Naipaul explored his thesis of a universal civilization most cogently. The novel opens with these words: "The world is what it is; men who are nothing, who allow themselves to become nothing, have no place in it."[29] Naipaul's forte is to browbeat his reader by such pontifical high writing. Where do you find these men he speaks about who are nothing? And what do you mean by nothing? Later in the story we find this:

> I asked for a cup of coffee. … It was a tiny old man who served me. And I thought, not for the first time, that in colonial days the hotel boys had been chosen for their small size, and the ease with which they could be manhandled. That was no doubt why the region had provided so many slaves in the old days: slave peoples are physically wretched, half-men in everything except in their capacity to breed the next generation.[30]

That is no longer merely troubling. I think it is downright outrageous. And it is also pompous rubbish. For those who may not be familiar with *A Bend in the River* I should mention that it is patterned on Conrad's *Heart of Darkness*. Perhaps Naipaul's title itself is an echo from Conrad's most dramatic passage where Marlow's steamer "struggled round a bend" as it "penetrated deeper and deeper into the heart of darkness." But while Conrad gives us an Africa of malignant mystery and incomprehensibility, Naipaul's method is to ridicule claims to any human achievement in Africa.

Naipaul's narrator, Salim, is an Indian shopkeeper whose forefathers had been brought by the British to work in their East African colonies in much the same way as Naipaul's people were taken to Trinidad. Salim's qualification for narrator of Naipaul's African story is rather slim. Although he had grown up in East Africa, he did not really know Africans; he had lived in a closed Indian community whose attitude was to look down on the Africans. Naipaul could have used this limitation to call the trustworthiness of Salim's narrative into question and, in that way, written a different kind of book. But he evidently had no such intention. He held Africans in deep contempt himself, and made no secret of it. Although he was writing about Africa, he was not writing for Africans. According to Caryll Phillips, Naipaul in a 1980 interview with *The New York Times* had said: "I don't count the

African readership and I don't think one should. Africa is a land of bush, again, not a very literary land." About Asians he wasn't much kinder. He said they do not read and that if they read at all it is for magic. About Trinidad, his original home country, he went totally overboard:

> I can't see a Monkey—you can use a capital M, that's an affectionate word for the general-ity—reading my work. No, my books aren't read in Trinidad now. … These people live purely physical lives which I find con-temptible. … It makes them interesting only to chaps in universities who want to do com-passionate studies about brutes.[31]

He doesn't pull his punches, does he? And so we would not expect him to be kind to Africa in *A Bend in the River*, and he isn't. Conrad's "great wall of vegetation," which has, at least, a kind of ambiguous grandeur, is now cut down to Naipaul's mere "bush"; Conrad's "black, incomprehensible frenzy" of the Africans to a rather pitiful rage that will try to set fire to concrete; and so on, and so on, and so on. Africa is a laughable place and ultimately of no account; a place where men have allowed themselves to become nothing. The real story of *A Bend in the River* is how an Indian shopkeeper doing business in the heart of Africa and with family connections in East Africa learns to break free from primitive ties to a doomed continent and make a dash for the bounties of the universal civilization in Europe and North America. His mentor, another Indian and an old classmate from East Africa days who has now come to Salim's town as a visiting scholar at the new polytechnic, has brought him a winning philosophy that demands total rejection of one's history. Its motto seems to be: Trample on the past!

> You trample on the past, you crush it. In the beginning it is like trampling on a garden. In the end you are just walking on ground. That is the way we have to learn to live now. The

past is here. (He touched his heart.) It isn't there. (And he pointed at the dusty road.)"[32]

Well, it is not true that my history is only in my heart; it is indeed there, but it is also in that dusty road in my town, and in every villager, living and dead, who has ever walked on it. It is in my country too; in my continent and, yes, in the world. That dusty little road is my link to all the other destinations. To ask everybody to shut down their history, pack their bag and buy a one-way ticket to Europe or America is just crazy, to my way of thinking. To suggest that the universal civilization is in place already is to be willfully blind to our present reality and, even worse, to trivialize the goal and hinder the materialization of a genuine universality in the future.

Letters from Home

The notion of restlessness, of the artist-in-exile has been very attractive to the western mind. The list of European and American painters and writers who have left home for some other country in this century and the one before is very impressive indeed. Let me mention an arbitrary half-dozen that come first to my mind—Picasso leaving Spain for Paris; Rimbaud leaving France for Abyssinia; Rilke changing homes twenty times in two years; even James Baldwin returning to America from France in a casket and W. E. B. Du Bois finding a resting place in Ghana. Diverse as their individual situations or predicaments were, these children of the West roamed the world with the confidence of the authority of their homeland behind them. The purchasing power of even very little real money in their pocket set against the funny money all around them might often be enough to validate their authority without any effort on their part.

The experience of a traveller from the world's poor places is very different, whether he is travelling as a tourist or struggling to settle down as an exile in a wealthy country. One could give a whole lot of time to that subject but I am not going to. Let me just say of such a traveller that he will not be able to claim a double citizenship like Gertrude Stein when she said: "I am an American and Paris is my hometown."

Perhaps it is just as well that travelling is tough for us. That way the chances are good that we will stay at home, or if we travel, will plan to return home as soon as possible. It is, of course, sad in the extreme that one is obliged to say this. People everywhere should be free and able to come and go at will. That time will surely come when it will become possible to do so. It is not here yet.

The brilliant Ghanian writer Ama Ata Aidoo wrote a short masterpiece, *Our Sister Killjoy*, in sequences of fine prose and muscular poetry, which explores the condition of African sojourners in London. The narrator is a bright young woman recently graduated from university in Ghana and selected for a short fellowship in Germany.

Her journey, for the first time outside

Africa, becomes a personal and a cultural rite of passage yielding sharp insights into her inner self and the strange world of Europe. When her short visit to Germany ends she is drawn—in spite of her rebellious political self—to the same London that Ghana had so recently freed herself from. And there she finds fellow Ghanaians who had completed their studies and found one excuse or another not to go home:

> They work hard for the
> Doctorates—
> They work too hard,
> Giving away
> Not only themselves, but
> All of us—
> The price is high,
> My brother,
> Otherwise the story is as old as empires.
> Oppressed multitudes from the provinces rush
> to the imperial seat because that is where they
> know all salvation comes from. But as other
> imperial subjects in other times and other

places have discovered, for the slave there is nothing at the centre but worse slavery.

The narrator's sharp eye then zooms in to capture the ragged appearance of West Africans and West Indians in London. And "she knew from one quick composite vision, that in a cold land, poverty shows as nowhere else."[33]

Ama Ata Aidoo does not pull her punches, either. But she is on the right side, on behalf of the poor and the afflicted, the kind of "nothing people" Naipaul would love to hammer into the ground with his well-crafted mallet of deadly prose.

The great Indian writer R. K. Narayan told Edward Blishen, English poet and broadcaster, his experience as a writer in India; how he would sometimes look out of his window and quickly walk away again because there were simply too many stories out there![34] Apparently he did not see a million mutinies like Naipaul; only a million stories clamoring to be told. And he has given a lifetime telling a good many of them in his un-fussy, half-comical, half-whimsical way that takes the reader, unawares, into enchanted territories of universal wisdom. He even invented an imaginary village in South India specifically for his stories and called it Malgudi. Narayan invested in India; he did not take himself out.

Nothing I have said in these remarks is aimed at writers whose lives may be in danger in their homes. It would be impertinent to presume to tell anyone in that situation what to do. I am concerned only with the advertisement of expatriation and exile as intrinsically desirable goals for the writer or as the answer to the problem of unequal development in the world. People have sometimes asked me if I have thought of writing a novel about America since I have now been living here some years. My answer has always been "No, I don't think so." Actually, living in America for some years is not the only reason for writing a novel on it. Kafka wrote such a novel without leaving Prague. No, my reason is that America has enough novelists writing about her, and Nigeria too few. And so it is, again, ultimately, a question of balance. You cannot balance one thing; you balance a diversity of things. And diversity is the engine of the evolution of living things, including living civilizations.

To any writer who is working in the remote provinces of the world and may now be contemplating giving up his room or selling his house and packing his baggage for London or New York I will say: Don't trouble to bring your message in person. Write it where you are, take it down that little dusty road to the village post office and send it!

In Cheikh Hamidou Kane's great novel of colonization, *Ambiguous Adventure*, a brilliant, young aristocrat and hope of his people is sent away from his muslim community in Senegal by the elders to study in Paris. Their decision, which was not reached without deep misgivings, was ultimately made possible by a vision of their son joining the sons of Europe and other continents to construct a new world for

all humanity. The young African, Samba Di-
allo, will, however, discover that, contrary to
the optimistic notions of his people, Europe
has made no real provision for his participation. That discovery that one is somehow su-
perfluous is there, waiting at journey's end, for
the weary traveller from the provinces. The
great metropolis is not your little village; it has
too many world-shaking concerns to be troubling itself about your insignificant homely
affairs. It may even not bring quickly to mind
exactly where the little province you say you
come from is located in the vastness of its territories, as happened to a prominent Nigerian
educator and social critic, the late Tai Solarin,
when he went as a student to London in the
1950s. He took a parcel to the post office for
dispatch to his people in Nigeria. A lady at the
counter took it from him and weighed it. To
do the calculation for postage she looked
again at the address and said: "Nigeria …
Nigeria … Is Nigeria ours or French?" To
which Solarin, a very austere man, replied:
"Nigeria is yours, madam." To even inconse-

quential minions of imperial rule, subject peoples were all "invisible," along with their sometimes unpronounceable homelands.

But changes have begun to occur. That exchange between the Nigerian, Tai Solarin, and the British postal worker could not happen today and, if it did, Solarin would have been glad of the educational opportunity to tell the good lady that, for good or ill, Nigeria was neither hers nor French but his.

That may not sound like a whole lot of progress; but it is a beginning. It is certainly enough to soften the great anxiety we had about that first postal establishment in my village and to remove the need for us to see the diligent postal worker as a licensed killer. We can even sit back and savor, perhaps with a wry smile on our faces, an incredible metaphoric transformation of the humble postman from the killer we called him to the healer Philip Larkin makes of him in his fine poem "Aubade," which achieves an amazing, bare-bones depiction of London at the hour of daybreak, when "telephones crouch, getting ready to ring / in locked-up offices" and "postmen like doctors go from house to house."[35]

A fine poem, "Aubade," about a great city, indeed my favourite among the world's great cities. But even so it must be quite apparent that relations between me and London cannot always have been easy. I remember very well the first day I set foot in London in early 1957, a young broadcaster from colonial Nigeria come to learn the profession of radio at the famous BBC staff school. It was a journey with too many firsts for comfort—my first journey out of Nigeria, my first-ever air travel and my first visit to England; and I was glad to be welcomed at the airport by someone familiar, indeed by my brother, an engineering student in London. He expertly found us a cab and I had my first taste of being chauffeured by a white man. I merely took note of this unimaginable event and said nothing. But London hadn't quite finished with me; it proceeded to unveil an even more unbelievable sight. At a minor traffic hold-up on our way, caused by road works, I saw a white man in dirty work clothes filling up cracks in the road with steaming asphalt. I had to talk to my brother then, in our secret language of course, over the head of the driver. My brother inured, it would seem, to such marvels laughed at my surprise and added: "If he goes to Nigeria tomorrow they will call him Director of Works."

That was London, the great metropolis that ruled my world from afar without letting me into any of these secrets, without admitting that, like me, it was also vulnerable. The next seven months, which I spent learning broadcasting and travelling in Britain, filled some more gaps in my perception of how things stood in the imperial scheme. One of the best memories I have of those months was the day, quite early in the course, when my class was taken out for a practical lesson in radio commentary, an aspect of broadcasting I did not particularly care for. I was set down at the foot of a bridge somewhere, a microphone was thrust into my hand and I was asked to tell an imaginary audience what was going on around me! All the help I was given was the information that across that bridge ahead of me was someplace called Middlesex. I did what I could. Many anxious days passed before the morning of reckoning when the instructor came back to review our performances, one by one. To my utter amazement he spoke particularly well of my effort, going so far as to suggest that my transparent lack of familiarity with the setting had given my commentary an exceptional quality of freshness and power, or words to that effect. I listened carefully for sarcasm and heard none.

I began to like London quite a bit after that. Perhaps only a mighty metropolis could have that bigness of heart, that confidence and the strength to be that magnanimous to a faltering stranger. But might such graciousness not carry at the same time a suggestion that London was perhaps a little dumb, too easy a dupe, too ready to fall prey to any wily wanderer from its distant, poverty-stricken provinces? Perhaps I could make a living here merchandising my inchoate perceptions of the city fabricated in the smithy of a gigantic unfamiliarity. But could I see myself taking that as my life's work? I would rather be where I could see my work cut out for me, where I could tell what I was looking at. In other words my hometown. And from there I would visit again when I could, happily without the trepidation I had had when I had imagined London to be all-powerful. Now I can talk without the harsh vocabulary that called the mail deliverer a killer. The dispossession that caused my shrillness is in retreat though the marks of its pillage are still everywhere. I can see, in spite of them, that I have come a long way.

By the way, the passport I carried on that first visit to London had defined me as a "British Protected Person." That was an arrogant lie because I never did ask anyone to protect me. And to protect someone without his request or consent is like the proverbial handshake that goes beyond the elbow and begins to look like kidnapping. Now my passport calls me a "Citizen of Nigeria." In today's circumstances Nigeria might not sound altogether like an unqualified piece of good news. But I have never thought it was. Which is precisely what it means to have my work cut out for me. To those who believe that Europe and North America have already invented a universal civilization and all the rest of us have to do is hurry up and enroll, what I am proposing will appear unnecessary if not downright foolish. But for others who may believe with me that a universal civilization is nowhere yet in sight, the task will be how to enter the preliminary conversations. My transition from British Protected Person to Nigerian Citizen is one man's participation in a monumental ritual by millions and millions to appease a long and troubled history of dispossession and bitterness, and to answer "present" at the rebirth of the world as the poet, Senghor, might say.

I referred earlier in these reflections, with complete approval, to Salman Rushdie's hap-

py characterization of the decolonizing process by the metaphor of postal correspondence. But when he goes on to say in
another context that "Literature has little or
nothing to do with a writer's home address,"[36] I just wonder if in seeking to free
the writer from all ties we might not end up
constraining literature's long reach into
every nook and corner of every writer's experience and imagining, including his encounter with the extraordinary invention
called the passport.

Notes

1   Joyce Cary, *Mister Johnson* (New York: New Directions, 1989), p. 138.
2   Cary, *Mister Johnson*, p. 99.
3   Dorothy Hammond and Alta Jablow, *The Africa that Never Was* (Prospect Heights, Ill.: Waveland Press, 1992), p. 20.
4   Hammond and Jablow, p. 21.
5   Basil Davidson, *The African Slave Trade* (Boston: Little, Brown, 1980), p. 29.
6   Hammond and Jablow, p. 22, 23.
7   Hammond and Jablow, p. 9.
8   F. J. Pedler, *West Africa* (London: Methuen & Co., 1951), p. 32.
9   Both quotes from Pedler, *West Africa*, p. 49; 50.
10 Hammond and Jablow, p. 20.

11   Joseph Conrad, *Heart of Darkness* (New York: W. W. Norton, 1988), p. 37.

12   Hammond and Jablow, p. 13.

13   Hammond and Jablow, p. 9.

14   Hammond and Jablow, p. 17.

15   Alan Hill, "British publishers' constructive contribution to African literature," *Logos* 3, no. 1 (1992): 45.

16   Dylan Thomas, "Blithe Spirits," *Sunday Observer*, July 6, 1952, quoted in *Critical Perspectives on Amos Tutuola*, ed. Bernth Lindfors (Washington D.C.: Three Continents Press), p. 8.

17   Elspeth Huxley, *Four Guineas* (London: Chatto and Windus, 1954), p. 175.

18   Both quotes are from Elspeth Huxley, *The Flame Trees of Thika* (London: Chatto and Windus, 1961), p. 8, quoted in Micere Githae-Mugo, *Visions of Africa* (Nairobi: Kenya Literature Bureau, 1978), p. 14.

19   West Africa April 10, 1954; June 5, 1954, quoted in Lindfors, *Critical Perspectives on Amos Tutuola*, p. 41.

20   Elspeth Huxley, *White Man's Country* (London: Chatto &Windus, 1935), vol. 1, p. 221, quoted in Githae-Mugo, p. 17.

21   Huxley, *White Man's Country*, quoted in Githae-Mugo, p. 15.

22   Jomo Kenyatta, *Facing Mount Kenya*, London: Secker and Warburg, 1938); reprinted in *African Short Stories*, ed. Chinua Achebe and C. L. Innes (Oxford: Heinemann, 1985), p. 36.

23   Kenyatta, *Facing Mount Kenya*, in *African Short Stories*, p. 39.

24 Kenyatta, *Facing Mount Kenya*, in *African Short Stories*, p. 39.

25 Githae-Mugo, p. 19.

26 Githae-Mugo, p. 20.

27 Dylan Thomas, "Wales and the Artist," Quite Early One Morning, BBC radio, 1954.

28 Buchi Emecheta, interivew by Adeola James, in *In Their Own Voices: African Women Writers Talk* (London: James Currey Ltd., 1990), p. 39.

29 V. S. Naipaul, *A Bend in the River* (New York: Vintage, 1989), p. 3.

30 Naipaul, *A Bend in the River*, p. 76.

31 Both quotes from an interview with V. S. Naipaul by Caryl Phillips, "The Voyage In," *New Republic* (June 13, 1994): 41.

32 Naipaul, *A Bend in the River*, p. 112.

33 Ama Ata Aidoo, *Our Sister Killjoy* (Reading, Mass.: Addison Wesley, 1997)

34 Edward Blishen, Chinua Achebe and Doris Lessing, A Good Read, BBC radio, January 1994.

35 Philip Larkin, "Aubade," *Collected Poems* (New York: Farrar, Straus, & Giroux, 1988), p. 209.

36 Rushdie, Salman, "Damme, this is the Oriental Scene for you," *New Yorker* (June 23, 30, 1997): 56.

Index

Index

ALSO BY CHINUA ACHEBE

GIRLS AT WAR AND OTHER STORIES

Girls at War and Other Stories reveals the essence of life in Nigeria and traces twenty years in the literary career of one of the twentieth century's most acclaimed writers. In this collection of stories, which display an astonishing range of experience, Chinua Achebe takes us inside the heart and soul of a people whose pride and ideals must compete with the simple struggle to survive. Hailed by critics everywhere, Achebe's fiction re-creates with energy and authenticity the major issues of daily life in Africa.

Fiction/Short Stories/0-385-41896-5

HOPES AND IMPEDIMENTS

Chinua Achebe here considers the place of literature and art in our society in a collection of essays spanning his best writing and lectures from the last several years. For Achebe, overcoming Eurocentrism in our appreciation of works of the imagination goes hand in hand with eradicating the destructive effects of racism and injustice in Western society. He reveals the impediments that still stand in the way of open, equal dialogue between Africans and Europeans, and between blacks and whites, but he also instills us with hope that they will soon be overcome.

Literary Criticism/Essays/0-385-41479-X

Also available:

Anthills of the Savannah, 0-385-26045-8

Arrow of God, 0-385-01480-5

A Man of the People, 0-385-08616-4

No Longer at Ease, 0-385-4745 5-5

Things Fall Apart, 0-385-47454-7

ANCHOR BOOKS
Available at your local bookstore, or call toll-free to order:
1-800-793-2665 (credit cards only).